"Looking For Dan:
The Puzzling Life of a Frontier Character-Daniel DuBois"

Best Wishes

John Lewis Taylor

John Lewis Taylor

First published by Dog Ear Publishing
4010 W. 86th Street, Ste H
Indianapolis, IN 46268
www.dogearpublishing.net

ISBN: 978-1-4575-3371-6

Library of Congress Control Number: has been applied for

This book is printed on acid-free paper.

Printed in the United States of America

Dan Dubois Moves West

*T*he American Southwest of the mid-nineteenth and early twentieth century was a magnet for young men seeking adventure. These men were analogous to Christopher "Kit" Carson, a saddler's apprentice who ran away from his workbench to become legendary frontiersmen, Indian agent, and Union General in the Civil War, the brothers William and Charles Bent, who built a trading and political empire in the early days of New Mexico and Colorado, and Lucien Maxwell who operated the largest land grant in the Southwest and established the first bank in New Mexico. The Southwest was a place where a youth could shape his destiny and reinvent himself. One of these adventurers was Dan Dubois, a man whose life remains a conundrum, a puzzle and a mystery, yet unsolved.

The story of Dan Dubois began March 7, 1835, at "Two Rivers Forked" plantation, near New Orleans, Louisiana, with Dan's birth to Santiago Dubois, an immigrant from France and Margaret Donovan who was a native of Ireland.[1] Santiago Dubois, in addition to being

[1] Baer, Peggy. ptbaer@gmail.com "Dan Notes" 2 August 2009, personal e-mail (2 August 2009).

a planter also dealt in slaves, and Daniel, even from an early age had issues with the institution of slavery. The Dubois family, according to a family legend told by Dan's grandson, Dan Dubois Garduno, was wealthy and young Dan was raised in luxury. Dan's opposition to slavery may have been one of the reasons that Dan left home as a youth and went, "Out West". [2]

Daniel Dubois's connection to a slave holding family is inferred by Southwestern anthropologist Fredrick Webb Hodge's short article "Old Dan Dubois", in which Hodge relates a story about John Shato; an African-American man who enters a saloon in Gallup, New Mexico, in 1899 and overhears Dan singing. He asks Dan to repeat the song, and says, "No one could sing that way but my old master, Dan Dubois." He and Dan embrace and Shato tells Dan that his mother, Mary Hilda, was Dan's old nurse and is still alive and living in St. Louis, Missouri.[3]

For whatever reason, dislike for slavery or love of adventure, Dan Dubois left his home and went west, when still a very young man. There are several stories of how Dan made his way to California. One story, says that he first went to St. Louis, Missouri, but did not care for the place and journeyed from there overland through New Mexico arriving in California sometime in the 1850s. In California, he became a noted rider and roper

[2] Garduno, Dan. Interview by Richard Rubi. Collection of Rosemarie "Shorty" Sandoval, 1974-1975.

[3] Hodge, Fredrick Webb. "Old Dan DuBois" Los Angeles Westerners Brandbook , 1950, 148 Autry National Center, Braun Research Library: Amelia Garduno to F.W. Hodge 11-16-1952

and a friend of the bandit Joaquin Murrieta. Early in his life, Dan joined a group of Apaches and traveled with them to the Mohave country. Dan told Hodge that living among the Mohave were two white girls and that he recalled that one was named Olive. Hodge was sure that Dan had crossed paths with the Oatman sisters, who were captured by the Yavapi in Arizona in 1851.[4] The sisters, Olive and Mary Ann were taken captive and their parents were killed in the attack; their brother Lorenzo was left for dead. Sometime later, the girls were adopted into a Mohave family named Espaniole.[5] Hodge felt that this story dated Dan's presence in California and Arizona and his age at the time, he went west. Hodge also felt that the story was true because Dan would have had no personal knowledge of the Oatman affair and was able to provide a great deal of detail concerning Mohave life.[6]

Just when Dan left the Apache is not known, but much later in life, he told Andrew Vanderwagen, an old friend and a missionary at Zuni, that he had lived with the Apache for a time and had an Apache wife and children.[7] Dan would maintain a close relationship with the Apache for most of his life, and Dan Garduno stated that his grandfather apparently felt that being surrounded by Apaches was the only way to live.[8]

[4] Hodge, "Old Dan DuBois", 139,140.
[5] Mifflin, Margot, "Olive Oatman White Mohave" Native Peoples Vol. XII. No. 1 Jan/Feb., 2010, 65-67.
[6] Hodge, "Old Dan DuBois", 140.
[7] Thomas, Elaine D. Shiwi Vander Wagens. (Zuni: Self published , 1997), 21
[8] Garduno: Interview

After leaving Apacheria and returning to California, Dan became interested in the fur trade, and with New Mexico Mountain man, Louis La Bodie traveled to Taos, New Mexico.[9] In an interview on April 25, 1889, Dan told the *Santa Fe New Mexican* that he first came to Santa Fe in 1851.[10] This visit must have been when Dan was on his way to California and passed through the New Mexico capitol. While in New Mexico Territory Dan became acquainted with Kit Carson and other famous frontiersmen. Moving from Taos, he was employed by the army as a dispatch rider at Fort Defiance, a military post in the Navajo country.[11]

On April 30, 1860, the Navajo, following a period of increasing friction with the United States, attacked Fort Defiance; the garrison was able to repel the attackers and maintain control of the fort. In the fall of 1860, more United States troops were sent to the Fort Defiance area and Colonel Edward R.S. Canby carried out a less than successful campaign to gain control of the region. It is not known if Dan Dubois took part in this action.[12] On April 25, 1861, the United States withdrew all of its forces from Fort Defiance as a part of the general withdrawals of military garrisons from posts on the frontier. The Civil War was on and the Lincoln administration needed the troops and resources from the western forts to aid in the suppression of Southern Independence

[9] Hodge, "Old Dan DuBois", 139
[10] Lauge, Riley, Lauge. The Southwest Journals of Adolph F. Bandelier 1889-1892. (Albuquerque: University of New Mexico Press, 1984), 351, 352.
[11] Hodge, "Old Dan DuBois", 139
[12] Locke, Raymond Friday. The Book of the Navajo (Los Angeles: Mankind Publishing Company, 2001, original 1976), 333-340.

Civil War Years

an Dubois, during the early years of the Civil War, according to family stories and William Moore in *Chiefs, Agents, and Soldiers*, lived with the Utes in Colorado.[13] Than sometime early in 1863, Dan returned to California and worked as a merchant seaman, sailing down the coast of Mexico to Chile, around Cape Horn to the east coast of the United States. He then left the sea and made his way to Ohio to enlist in the Union Army.[14]

For reasons known only to Dan, he enlisted under the name Dennis Donovan in Company I. 129th Ohio Volunteer Infantry on May 4, 1863,; he was given the rank of Private and the duty of a teamster. Company I under the command of Captain Xenophan Wheeler left Camp Taylor in Ohio for Camp Nelson in Kentucky. The unit marched through Kentucky to Tazewell, Tennessee, and was assigned watch duty along the Clinch River. The military need for this posting was to keep secure the

---

[13] Moore, William Haas. Chiefs, Agents, and Soldiers. (Albuquerque: University of New Mexico Press, 1994), 110.
[14] Dubois, Dan. "Sworn Statement before a Notary, McKinley County, New Mexico. May 1, 1922.""

Cumberland Gap. The 129th's post and picket duty was difficult and they lost twenty-five soldiers to disease and exposure.[15] When the 129th was relieved from duty, the unit returned to Camp Taylor and Private Donovan was discharged on November 8, 1863.[16]

After discharge, Dennis remained in the East and lived for a time in New York City. On September 6, 1864, he enlisted in the United States Navy at Camden, New Jersey. His age at this time is listed as 27 and his birthplace in given as Ireland. He was assigned to serve on the *Princeton* and given the duty of a coal heaver. Seaman Donovan would serve on the *New Hampshire*, the *Camellia*, and the *North Carolina*. The mission of these vessels was to perform picket duty as part of the Union blockade of Confederate ports.[17]

[15] Stevens, Larry. "129th Ohio Infantry" www.ohiocivilwar.com/cw129.htm. 03-09-2005.

[16] United States War Department, Volunteer Service record of Dennis Donovan 129th Ohio Volunteer Infantry.

[17] C.B. Hatch to Commissioner of Pensions, Donovan, Dennis ex Coal Heaver, Pension Claim, July 3, 1924.

Back to the Southwest

*S*oon after Dennis's service in the Union Navy ended in July of 1865, he returned to the Southwest and again became Dan Dubois. At first, he rejoined the Utes in Colorado and accompanied them on raids against the Cheyenne on the plains of eastern Colorado. For a time, using his experience as a teamster, he drove a stagecoach route from Denver to Santa Fe for Ben Holladay the stagecoach magnate.[18] Dan's next employment was with Lucien Maxwell the owner of the vast Maxwell land grant in northern New Mexico and later the owner of Fort Sumner. [19]

It was while Dan was in Maxwell's service that he met Rosa the youngest daughter of the Navajo leader Manuelito.[20] Rosa was a servant to the Maxwell family and a genizaro. Genizaros were a class of Native people who as children were stolen in slave raids, usually by

[18] Telling, Irving. "New Mexico Frontiers: A Social History of the Gallup Area 1881-1891" (Cambridge, MA.: Doctoral Thesis at Harvard University, 1952), 29.
[19] Baer, e-mail, "Dan Notes"
[20] Juarez, Tony. tps50@msn.com "Rosa Manuelito" 23 November 2012, personal e-mail (23 November 2012)

hostile tribes and sold to Hispanic settlers. They became servants or agricultural serfs.[21]

Dubois's descendants tell many different stories as to how Rosa became the property of the Maxwells. One version is that Maxwell's men actually took part in raids against Native villages and carried off Rosa.[22] Another story states that Rosa was captured by the Utes and then later sold to the Maxwells. It is known that Lucien Maxwell and other Anglo New Mexicans obtained Native slaves in this manner. One example is Deluvina Maxwell a Navajo from Canyon De Chelly who was purchased from the Utes by Lucien Maxwell. Deluvina became a household servant to Maxwell's wife and later to his daughter Paulette, who became famous for being the girlfriend of Billy the Kid.[23]

During the time that Dan and Rosa were with the Maxwells, Rosa had two children, Joaquin and Guadalupe (aka Lupe).[24] A story related by Dan himself to Hodge at a banquet held in Gallup, New Mexico, linked Dan's daughter, Lupe, to the Maxwell family. Dan pointed out a young woman in the crowd and said to Hodge, "See that gal? Well, she has always thought she's my daughter, but she's really the daughter of Charlie Maxwell." Later it was explained to Hodge that Charlie was the brother of Lucien Maxwell.[25] This story is seem-

[21] Silverman, Jason. "Indian Slavery: The Gernizaros in New Mexico." Native Peoples. July/August 2011, 50-53.

[22] Baer, e-mail, 08-10-2009.

[23] Moore, Chiefs, Agents, and Soldiers, 267.

[24] Juarez, e-mail, 11-23-12.

[25] Hodge, "Old Dan DuBois"., 144.

ingly contradicted by the historic record because Lucien Maxwell had only one brother, Ferdinand. However, many of Maxwell's employees and servants took the family name; there is the possibility that there was a Charlie "Maxwell".[26] And many of Dan's descendants except as fact that Lupe was a Maxwell and cite her as Lupe Maxwell in family genealogical records.[27] In addition to Joaquin and Lupe, Dan and Rosa had another child, a daughter Amelia, who was born in the mid-1870s in Trinidad, Colorado.[28]

At some point Dan grew tired of working for the Maxwells, and one day told Lucien Maxwell that he was taking Rosa and the children home to the Navajo country and reminding him that slavery in New Mexico Territory and the rest of the United States was now illegal. Then without further ceremony, Dan loaded up a wagon and drove off the Maxwell ranch.[29]

[26] Freiberger, Harriet, Telephone interview with John Lewis Taylor, 02-02-2011.

[27] www.rubifamilygen.net.
www.familysearch.org. There is a Rose Maxwell listed in the 1870 U.S Census for New Mexico Territory, Colfax County with post office at Elizabeth City. She is listed as age 20 and born in the "Navajo Country" also a Jaukin age 2 and Lupita Maxwell age 5 months are listed, they are shown as being born in New Mexico. The census does not show that Jaukin and Lupita are related to Rose, but the three are the only Maxwells listed in the household of Jon Armenta. The time and place for all three fits the life of Rosa Manuelito.

[28] Autry, A. Garduno to F.W. Hodge, March 01, 1950.

[29] Baer, e-mail, 08-10, 2009.

Life in Navajo Country

After leaving the Maxwells, Dan returned to the Navajo Country and found work as a Spanish language interpreter. Dan Dubois's work as an interpreter at Fort Defiance soon involved him in a power struggle between the Indian Agent to the Navajo William F.M. Arny and Thomas V. Keam.[30]

Thomas Varker Keam was born in England the son of a sea captain. He joined the English Merchant Marines as a young man and docked in San Francisco in time for the American Civil War. Soon after his arrival, Keam joined the California Volunteers of the Union Army and after several weeks of training, the column, under the command of James Henry Carlson, began its long march to protect New Mexico Territory from Confederate invasion and to safeguard the Southwestern frontier.

By the time the troops reached the Rio Grand, the Confederates had returned to Texas and there was little sign they would return. General Carlson, soon after

---

[30] McNitt, Frank. The Indian Traders. (Norman: University of Oklahoma Press, 1962). 156.
Correll, Lee J. "Events In Navajo History" The Navajo Times No. 20, March 2, 1967.

establishing himself in Santa Fe, began his campaign against the Mescalero Apache and the Navajo in order to secure the vast region of New Mexico and western Texas.

Thomas Keam was assigned to Fort Sumner to help retain the Apache and Navajo who were being rounded-up and relocated on the Bosque Redondo reservation. During his service here, Keam developed knowledge of the Navajo language and an interest in the Navajo people. By 1869 Thomas Keam was out of military service and was employed as an interpreter at Fort Defiance, and in the same year he married Asdzaan Liba , a Navajo woman of the Ashee'hi clan who had not gone to Fort Sumner. Keam proved to be popular with the Navajo and with the military at Fort Wingate, and so with the death of Agent James H. Miller in 1872 Thomas Keam was appointed acting Agent to the Navajo.[31]

Ulysses S. Grant, as president of the United States, sought to reform Indian Policy, end abuse and corruption in the Indian Service, and bring the gifts of civilization to the native peoples. A tool for meeting these goals was to contract the day-to-day operation of Indian Affairs to the various Christian Churches and their reform movements. The Navajo were placed under the Presbyterian Board of Foreign Missions. Many of the Agency employees who were employed with the Presbyterian Board objected to Keam and other agency employees who lived with Navajo women. This faction wrote strong letters to John Lowrie the director of the Presbyterian Board against

[31] Graves, Laura. Thomas Varker Keam Indian Trader. (Norman: University of Oklahoma Press, 1998), 27-41.

Keam, Dan Dubois, and others stating that they were an unfit example to the Indians and so in September 1873, Lowrie replaced Keam with William Frederick Milton Arny as Agent to the Navajo.[32]

Arny was an abolitionist who had worked for the Free Soil Movement in Kansas in the 1850s and campaigned for Abraham Lincoln in Illinois in 1860. He had experience in Indian affairs having served as agent to the Utes and Jicarilla Apaches, during 1862-1863; he was Secretary of New Mexico Territory and Special Agent to the Indians of New Mexico and in 1866, served as interim Governor of New Mexico Territory.[33]Arny, his resume aside, had serious flaws in character; he was a self-righteous bigot, an egomaniac, and none too honest when it came to administering government property. He was, in the opinion of historian Raymond Friday Locke, "the worst agent the Navajo ever had to contend with."[34]

Soon after taking his post, Arny issued a statement declaring that, "Any white man who married an Indian was a lost soul and unfit to remain in the presence of decent white men." He then discharged Thomas V. Keam, his brother William, Jesus Arviso, Anson Damon, Perry Williams, Charles Hardison, William Clark, W.W. Owens, and Daniel Dubois, from the agency as consequence of their promiscuous cohabitation with Navajo women.[35]

[32] Graves, Thomas Keam, 69-91.
[33] Cozzens, Peter. The Struggle for Apacheria Vol. I.(Mechanicsburg, PA: Stackpole Books, 2001) 649.
[34] Locke, Book of the Navajo, 398.
[35] Graves, Thomas Keam, 70.

During the upheaval that followed the expulsion of the "Squaw Men", Arny accused Dan Dubois of spreading rumors that if the Navajo rebelled against Arny, Thomas Keam would be appointed agent. Arny also accused Dubois of being drunk and defiant at the agency buildings and refusing to leave when asked.[36] Agent Arny was able to enlist U.S. District Attorney Thomas B. Catron to charge Dan Dubois, William Keam, and Anson Damon with selling liquor to the Navajo. This case dragged on until the spring of 1877 when all of the defendants were cleared of the charge.[37]

Arny's methods and misuse of government property put him in conflict with Navajo leaders. After an ill-fated trip to Washington D.C. with Arny, Navajo leaders had had enough and petitioned that the Indian Bureau replace Arny with Thomas Keam of whom the Navajos said, "he having been our agent, understanding our language, and knowing our wants, we place the utmost confidence in him." Dan served as Spanish interpreter for this petition and Rosa, signing the name Marie de la Rosa, below Dan's, was the Navajo interpreter, Anson Damon signed as a witness.[38] This petition, along with a second petition failed to get the results the Navajos were looking for, so when Arny was away on yet another trip to Washington D.C., they seized control of the agency.[39]

---

[36] McNitt, The Indian Traders, 165.
[37] Graves, Thomas Keam, 77.
[38] Correll, "Events in Navajo History" The Navajo Times, March 2, 1967.
[39] McNitt, The Indian Traders, 156.

When Arny returned to Santa Fe, he realized the situation was hopeless and resigned saying, "I have every reason to believe that Thomas V. Keam has consorted with William Keam, Anson C. Damon and Daniel Dubois and informed the Indians that he, Thomas V. Keam was to be their agent, and excited them to rebel against the Government."

Arny's successor was not Keam, however, but rather Alex Irvine, who reported to Washington D.C. in June 1876 that the "Squaw Men" were living near the reservation. He reported that Dan Dubois was still living with a Navajo woman and three or four children about one half mile from the reservation, but that he had no reason to complain about any of these parties. [40]

[40] McNitt, The Indian Traders, 164.

Ranch Life in the Territories

*F*ollowing his employment at Fort Defiance and his acquittal of the charge of selling liquor to Indians, Dan began ranching at Deer Springs (Ojo Del Venador), near the town of St. Johns in Apache County, Arizona Territory.[41] Soon after giving birth to a daughter, Amelia, Rosa Manuelito died. However, Rosa was properly the Navajo woman living with Dan in Agent Alex Irvine's report of June 1876. According to Amelia her mother died at La Pareda, New Mexico, that place located between Bluewater and Chavez, New Mexico.[42]

The 1880 United States Census for Apache County lists Daniel Dubois as the head of household, and Dan's new wife 20-year-old Dorotea , Joaquin, Guadalupe, and Amelia, Dan's children by Rosa Manuelito as living at the home. Dorotea is almost certainly Dan's second wife, Dorotea Ercorcia of Cubero, New Mexico whom he married at Old Fort Wingate, in Catholic ceremony, officiated by Father John Brun, a local priest from San Rafael, New Mexico in 1887. Also living in the household are Tomasa

---

[41] McNitt, The Indian Traders, 165.
[42] Autry, A Garduno to F.W. Hodge, June 6, 1950
www. rubifamilygen.net, Amelia Garduno aka Mele, 12-04-2012

Gonzales, her daughter Rosa and Rosa's children Thomasina and Luberto Gonzales. Richard Rubi a descendent of Dan's states that Rosa was Dorotea's mother and that Thomasina and Luberto were her siblings.[43]

Dan's ranch at Deer Springs was within the area claimed by the Apache leader Victorio who often raided the isolated ranches south of the new Fort Wingate. Dan's past association with the Apache kept him and his family fairly safe from these raids. Dan's grandson, Dan Garduno said his mother Amelia remembered several visits by bands of Apache who would stop off to see Dan and his Navajo children. These visits Garduno said terrified the Mexican women who lived at the ranch. On one visit, an Apache warrior gave Amelia a gray woolen blanket and after the Apaches left, her brother Joaquin examined it and found it stained with human blood. Garduno said that even after the blanket was washed his mother would never use it because she knew the Apaches had cut some poor Mexican woman's throat to obtain it.[44]

In September 1879, a young anthropologist named Frank Hamilton Cushing arrived at the pueblo of Zuni as a member of a "collecting party" sponsored by the newly created Bureau of American Ethnology. He stayed at the pueblo for four years, during which time he became a participant-observer of contemporary Zuni culture and was eventually initiated into the tribe.[45] Sometime during the early years of his residency, he became acquainted with Dan Dubois.

[43] www. ancestry.com, 1880 United States Census for Saint John Village, Apache County, Arizona Territory
[44] Garduno, Interview.

Cushing's first written communication with Dubois came in a letter dated July 25, 1880, when he wrote Dan concerning a conflict with the Zuni during their quadrennial pilgrimage to a sacred Zuni religious site located in east-central Arizona..[46] Dan's ranch was on the pilgrimage route and Dan had built a brush fence to enclose a part of his property. When confronted with this obstacle, the Zuni pilgrims set it afire. Dan was upset and according to his grandson Dan Garduno, "lassoed a Zuni high priest and dragged him behind his horse."[47] In response, several of the Zunis pulled pistols on Dan. A few days later Dan filed a complaint against two Zuni, Juan Tomas and Patrico in Apache County, Arizona Territory charging them with doing malicious damage to his property and behaving in a rude and threatening manner and with a display of firearms.[48] Cushing's letter explained the Zuni's case to Dan in an attempt to defuse the situation. Cushing said that the Pueblo Governor and Alcalde (head tribal official) were willing to repair Dan's fence, but would not make any further atonement because Dan had fired two pistol shots at the party, had thrashed one of its members and as Cushing pointed out, disturbed a most sacred religious rite. The Indians, Cushing said, held no grudge and he wrote. "I hope that you will have at once the kindness and good sense to consider their offer to make good your fence sufficient reparation."[49]

[45] Dodge, William A. Black Rock: A Cultural Landscape and the Meaning of Place. (Jackson: University Press of Mississippi, 2007) , 43.
[46] Green, Jesse ed. Cushing At Zuni: The Correspondence and Journals of Frank Hamilton Cushing 1879-1884
(Albuquerque: University of New Mexico Press, 1990), 118.
[47] Garduno, Interview.
[48] Hodge, "Old Dan DuBois", 143.
[49] Green, Cushing At Zuni, 118.

Dubois conflict with the Zuni Pueblo would come to figure in a court case someone hundred years later in "United States, Zuni Pueblo v. Earl Platt" which would establish the Pueblo's right to cross private property during their pilgrimage. It seems that Dan was the only rancher on the pilgrimage route to have a conflict with the Zuni pilgrims until Earl Platt in the 1980s.[50]

In spite of the conflict with Zuni, Cushing and Dan became friends and Dan was so taken with Cushing that he named his two daughters after Cushing's wife Emily and her sister Maggie. Cushing and his wife were also the godparents of Dan's daughter Emily.[51]

Although Dan had friendly relations with the Apache leader Victorio, his ranch was apparently not always safe from raids by other Apache groups. During a six-week period in the summer of 1881, the aged Apache leader Nana began a raid into New Mexico and was able to avoid a force of over one thousand U.S. Calvary and some two hundred civilian volunteers. Nana and his band fought over a dozen engagements, and with fewer than one hundred warriors killed fifty Americans, and captured a great deal of livestock, mainly horses and cattle, before vanishing into the Sierra Madre of Mexico. [52]

[50] Phoenix New Times, "Platt's Last Stand", March 8, 1989.
Zuni Tribe Lands Bill Hearings.,www.content.lib.utah.edu/cgi-bin/showfile.eye/csorout=/
[51] Autry, Emily Dubois to F.W. Hodge, March 16, 1950
Green, Cushing At Zuni, 377.
[52] Terrell, John Upton. Apache Chronicle. (New York: World Publishing, 1972). , 346-349.
Cozzens, The Struggle for Apacheria, 663.

One of the engagements of Nana's great raid was reported in *The Budget* a Milburn, New Jersey newspaper in 1886 and is entitled "An Adventure in Zuni". The account begins in August of 1881, shortly after group of rustlers stole a large herd of cattle from the Pueblo of Zuni and nearby ranchers. The Zuni and the ranchers select Dan Dubois to form and lead a posse to pursue and capture the rustlers and recover the livestock. In the pueblo at this time is a group of young men who are conducting a survey for the Territory of New Mexico and these men are asked to provide their long guns to the Zuni men who are in the posse, because the Indians are poorly armed having only pistols. The men hand over their rifles and shotguns to the Zuni and the posse leaves on its search.

"The posse is absent from the village for only a short time when the cry of, "Apaches! Apaches!" was raised by lookouts on the roofs of the pueblo. One of the surveyors, identified as Stonewall W by the newspaper, fears for Dan's wife and daughter and rides out to their ranch, located about three miles from the pueblo, with the intent of bringing them back to Zuni.[53] When Stonewall reaches the ranch, he finds Dan's sixteen-year-old daughter sitting in the doorway of the ranch house playing the guitar while her mother is busy with housework. Stonewall, speaking in Spanish, orders the women to run for their lives for safety in the village. Dan's daughter,

[53] This could not have been Dan's ranch at Deer Springs which was located over twenty miles from Zuni Pueblo
www.davidrumsey.com/maps5457.html July 1, 2013

looking at Stonewall with scorn, takes a rifle down from its place on the wall and speaking in Spanish to the surveyor says, "I will not run, I will fight them here!" Stonewall, Dan's daughter, and his wife, bolt the door of the house, climb to the roof, and began firing on the Apache raiders.

The fight grows more intense when Stonewall notices a single rider dashing through the Apaches and approaching the house. It is Dan Dubois, who joins his family in the defense of their home. Soon, the rest of the posse arrives and drive the raiders away.

Once it was clear that the Apache are gone, Dan and the posse herded the recovered cattle into the village and rejoin the pursuit of Nana's band."[54] This is where the account in the *Budget* ends, but Dan's group may have joined a force made up of companies I and K of the ninth cavalry who rode out from Fort Wingate, New Mexico in pursuit of Nana. These units were divided into detachments of about twenty men each and were under the command of Capt. Charles Parker and Lt. Henry H. Wright. As the force from Fort Wingate grew closer to the Apache, they broke down into small units because they could more effectively patrol the large area in which the hostiles were operating. On August 9, six days after the battle of Monica Springs, Lt. Wright's force joined Lt. Guilfoye's unit and continued the pursuit of Nana, but were unable to find the Apaches. However, Capt. Parker's nineteen men from company K made contact with Nana's band along the Rio Salado near Carrizo Canyon.

[54] "An Adventure in Zuni." The Budget. Millburn, NJ. , August 20, 1886

The troopers attacked but after a brief fight Nana's band slipped away. Lt. Guilfoye and his buffalo soldiers, Indian scouts and civilian volunteers were exhausted, out of supplies, and were unable to prevent the escape.[55]

In another story told by his grandson, Dan Garduno, Dan joins a campaign against Geronimo. Once on a lone scout in Apacheria Dan heard cries of pain. Approaching the source carefully, Dan saw a group of Apache women torturing a male Hispanic captive. The women blinded the man and staked him out over a slow fire. Every so often, one to the women would plaster the man's head with mud to keep him conscious. Dubois told his grandson that the women were having a great time, each trying to out do the other one another in inflicting pain on the poor Mexican.

Dan chose the right moment and charged the bevy on horseback, the women surprised and unarmed, scattered from the scene. Dan made sure they were gone and returned to the victim. The poor man begged to shoot him and said to Dubois in Spanish, "For hope of the salvation of your soul as a Christian and the milk you suckled from your mother's breast end my agony and go before they return." Dan did not hesitate; he put the poor man out of his misery with one pistol shot to the head and spurred his horse into a run, making his escape before the arrival of Apache warriors.[56]

During his years ranching at Deer Springs, Dan was involved in many other adventures; these adventures

[55] Lekson, Stephen H. Nana's Raid. (El Paso: Texas Western Press, 1987), 20, 21.
[56] Garduno, Interview.

reflect the tension between the several factions struggling for control of Apache County.[57]

On June 24, 1882, a fiesta was being held in St. Johns to honor the patron saint of the village, Saint John the Baptist. A major attraction of the fiesta was a Mexican circus with a troupe of acrobats. The town was packed with people there to enjoy the show and other activities. However, this gathering of people brought together two of the feuding factions of Apache County, sheep ranchers and cowboys from the Greer Ranch. The Greers were a family of Texans who located in Apache County shortly after the Civil War and were in conflict with the local, mostly Hispanic, sheep ranchers. The Greer Ranch cowboys, it was said, cut an ear off each sheepherder they caught on Greer grazing land. [58] Everything was going fine at the circus until one of the cowboys thought it would be funny to shoot the rope that held up the trapeze of an acrobat. The cowboy was successful and the trapeze artist fell to the ground. Then as Garduno said, "All hell broke loose!"

The crowd attacked the cowboys and they retreated to a house on the edge of town and prepared to make a fight of it. The sheep ranchers were determined to dislodge the cowboys and began shooting into the shack, and planned to plant black powder charges around the building hoping to blow the Texans "sky high".

[57] Garduno, Interview.
[58] Blue, Martha, Indian Trader the Life and Times of J.L. Hubbell. (Walnut, CA. Kiva Publishing, 2000), 68, 69.
Udall, Camerson. Images of American: St. Johns. (Charleston, SC.: Arcadia Publishing, 2008). , 40-43.

At this point, Dan Dubois arrived on the scene; he was in town for the fiesta and was enjoying a drink or two in a local saloon when a sheepherder asked his help in dealing with the Greers. According to an eyewitness, Dan walked up to the front door of the building, with bullets hitting around his feet and walked in. He offered the cowboys his personal pledge of safe conduct if the Texans would give up their weapons. The Texans took Dan up on his offer and tossed their firearms out of the front door. Dan then he escorted the cowboys out of town. With peace restored, the fiesta resumed and Dan returned to the saloon to finish his drink.[59]

During his years at Deer Springs, Dan also worked as a freighter, perhaps for Solomon Barth who ran a freight line from Cubero, New Mexico, to St. Johns, Arizona, by way of Zuni Pueblo. Barth also ran a hotel and store in St. Johns and traded with the Zuni selling them goods from his freight wagons.[60] Once again, Dan Garduno tells a story that takes place when the freight wagons driven by Dan Dubois and other teamsters join the wagon train of a wealthy merchant named Don Pitacio. In addition to his wagons and goods, Pitacio had several Indian women in his caravan. During the course of the day, Pitacio treated these women very badly, hitting them often and calling them crude and insulting names.

[59] Garduno, Interview.
[60] Udall, St. Johns, 13,14,15,25.
"Solomon Barth 1842-1928" (St. Johns, AZ.: Unpublished manuscript in the collection of the St. Johns and Apache County, Arizona Family History Center, 1998). ,5.

When the wagons stopped for the night, Dan and his friends made camp and were enjoying their evening meal. However, their meal was disturbed by Pitacio yelling insults at one of the women and beating her. "Let's hang the son of a bitch", Dan said, and he and his men walked over to Pitacio's camp took him prisoner, threw a rope over a tree limb, put a noose around his neck, and stood him on a barrel.

Don Pitacio had all night to beg for mercy and to think about his misdeeds. The next morning Dubois took him down and told him that if he every heard of him treating a woman badly again he would find him and hang him for sure. For the remainder of the time Dan and his friends were with the wagon train, Don Pitacio was a changed man he treated the women considerately and even let them ride in the wagons during the heat of the day.[61]

In 1883, Frank Hamilton Cushing wrote a letter to Dan Dubois introducing him to well known Swiss archaeologist Adolph F. Bandelier. In the letter Cushing told Dan that Bandelier could converse with him in Spanish, French or English and that he was on his way to Mexico to examine all ancient ruins of interest, he came across. Cushing went on to ask that Dan and his son Joaquin take the time to show Bandelier around the area. Using Cushing's letter of introduction Dan Dubois began working for Bandelier at Zuni. Bandelier employed Dan as a guide to help him locate ruins in the vicinity of his Deer Springs ranch. Dan was very knowledgeable of the

[61] Garduno, Interview.

region guiding Bandelier to sites along the Rio Concho. In his 1883, journal, Bandelier described Dan as a Californian who had been married to a Navajo woman and had three children by her. Bandelier went on to say that Dan's current wife was a Mexican who visited the camp. Bandelier noted that Dan was bitter against the Zuni, although, Dubois said they never molested him. Bandelier did not remark on the reasons for Dubois's low regard for the Zunis, although it may be speculated to be related to the fence-burning incident of 1880.[62]

[62] Lange, Riley, Lange. The Southwest Journals of Adolph F. Bandelier 1883-1884. (Albuquerque: University of New Mexico Press, 1970), 51,73,74,75,76.

The Pyramid Springs Homestead

*I*n April of 1884, Dan Dubois filed for a homestead on the Whitewater Wash south of Two Wells in what is now the Chi Chil Tah chapter (Cousins, New Mexico) of the Navajo Nation.[63] In the 1880s the main wagon road from Fort Defiance to Zuni ran along the Whitewater. The location was perfect for a trading post, to serve both Navajo and Zuni customers, and Dan took advantage of the opportunity. First, though he needed to earn enough money to buy stock for his new ranching venture, and so he went to work for George Washington Sampson, a veteran trader who owned several trading posts in the Navajo country.[64] According to historians Martin Link and Frank McNitt, Dan may have worked for Sampson at his post at Rock Springs, which is located north of Gallup.[65]

---

[63] Daniel Dubois Homestead Papers, U.S. Department of the Interior, October 22, 1904.

[64] Kelley, Klara. <kblelley47@yahoo.com. "Dan Dubois" 07 Jan. 2012 personal e-mail, (07 Jan. 2012).

Kelley, Klara and Harris Francis. " Navajoland Trading Posts", January, 2011.

[65] McNitt, Frank. Navajo Wars: Military Campaigns, Slave Raids, and Reprisals. (Albuquerque: University of New Mexico Press, 1972), 218.

Link, Martin, interview with John Lewis Taylor (Gallup, NM). July 13, 2010.

Dan's homestead was known as Pyramid Springs or Coyote Springs and would remain his home for the rest of his life. Dan proved out his homestead in 1905, having made the necessary improvements, cultivated ten acres where he always raised a crop and built a log cabin, outbuildings and several corrals. Sometime during his ownership of Pyramid Springs, Dan sold a 1/6 interest in his ranch to Nathan Bibo of Grants and St. Johns and 1/3 interest to Octaviano Telles of Gallup.[66]

In 1915, the United States government bought the property from Dubois, Bibo and Telles for the benefit of the Navajo Tribe. Many of Dan's Navajo descendants received Indian allotments nearby, including Lupe Maxwell Dubois, Dan's daughter.[67] Amelia Dubois, Dan's other daughter by Rosa Manuelito and her Hispanic husband Antonio Garduno took a homestead in the same area the property eventually passing to Dan D. Garduno[68]

During the late 1880s as Dan was quite busy developing his ranch on the Whitewater and working for Sampson, but he did have time to accept a job with his friend Cushing. In 1888, Frank Hamilton Cushing hired Dan as the camp utility man for the Hemenway Expedition. Dan's job was to look after the camp, wrangle the draft animals and from his ranch, provide the expedition with beef.[69] The Hemenway Expedition to the Southwest

[66] Kelley, Klara. "Miscellaneous Report on Pyramid Springs", August 23, 2010.
[67] Kelley, Klara. Kbkelly47@yahoo.com "Review Copy of Dan Dubois20 March 2013, personal e-mail (3 March 2013
[68] Kelley, Klara and Harris Francis. " Field Notes KF0401", April 1, 2011.
[69] Hodge, "Old Dan DuBois", 141.
Lauge, Riley, Lauge. Journals of Bandelier 1888-1889., 351-353.

was conceived by Cushing, and funded by Mary Hemen-way, a Boston philanthropist who had an interest in his-toric preservation and archeology. The multi-disciplinary expedition focused on the ethnology, the anthropology, the history and the archaeology of the American South-west, focusing on New Mexico in 1886, Arizona in 1887, and Zuni Pueblo in 1888. The Hemenway Expedition was staffed by the leading figures in their discipline of that period: Dr. Herman F. e. ten Kate, Dr. Adolf Bande-lier, Charles Garlick, and Dr. Frederick Webb Hodge.[70]

Dr. ten Kate described Dubois in his, *Diary of the Hemenway Expedition* as being a man of Herculean build and whose life is worthy of a "book hero" of the Wild West. "I," ten Kate said, "get the impression that the Indi-ans stand in awe of him; they respect him for his earlier acts of prowess and yet I notice a true-heartedness, almost tenderness in him sometimes."[71]

In the spring of 1889, Dan traveled to Santa Fe to meet with his old friend and employer, Adolph Bandelier. His visit was noted in the *Santa Fe Daily New Mexican* of April 25, 1889, saying that Mr. Dubois was staying at the Exchange Hotel and is having a "bushel of fun" talking over old times with the friends of other days. Dan, the report said, made his first visit to Santa Fe in 1851, com-ing from California that and he for the past several years had made his home with the Navajo. " These Indians", Dan told the reporter, "are prospering now as never

[70] Graves, Thomas Keam, 156.
[71] Ten Kate, Herman. Hemenway Expedition Diary 1887-1888. 635-689.

before; they have fine farms, droves of horses and are now engaged in the peaceful pursuit of shearing a million or so sheep." "Mr. Dubois", in the view of the reporter, "is one of that genial, brave hearted, stalwart type of frontiersman that has made the great west of today. But for such as he, civilization could never have crossed the Rockies. He talks of Tom Tobin, Kit Carson and 'old' Fifer and their adventures as few men now living can talk." The article went on to say that Dan was a linguist speaking French, German, Navajo, Apache, Spanish, and six Pueblo languages. [72]

Unfortunately, Dan's meeting with Bandelier did not go well due to the fact that Dan showed up at their meeting so fearfully drunk that he could not get a single straight word from him. [73]

Soon after Dan's work with the Hemenway Expedition ended, He began his career as an Indian trader. According to anthropologist Klara Kelley, Dan owned and operated a trading post at Pyramid Springs on his ranch in Chichiltah Chapter.[74] It is clear that Dan was not a major player as an Indian Trader, in this small store south of Gallup. Hodge notes in "Old Dan DuBois", that the post "had few patrons, most of which were the staff of the Hemenway Expedition".[75] The archaeologist Neil Judd visited the store in 1921, and wrote in his book *Men*

[72] Lauge, Riley, Lauge. Journals of Bandelier 1889-1892., 284.
Gallup Gleaner   May 1, 1889.
[73] Lauge, Riley, Lauge. Journals of Bandelier 1889-1892., 65.
[74] Kelley, Karla. Interview with John Lewis Taylor (Gallup NM) August 5, 2010.
[75] Hodge, "Old Dan DuBois", 145,146.

Met Along the Trail, that he found nothing on the store shelves but soda crackers and a few cans of axle grease.[76] In *Sagebrush Lawyer*, former Gallup mayor and New Mexico governor Arthur T. Hannett said that Dan ran a store near the Zuni line and that he and Benjamin Doc Sylvester, another old time Zuni trader, would once a year bring a pack train into Gallup to buy supplies for their stores.[77] Charles F. Lummis the well-known Southwestern adventurer and then editor of the *Los Angeles Times* stopped at DuBois's store while traveling from Zuni to the railhead at Manuelito Canyon. Lummis wrote, "When we reached the comfortable casa of Dan Dubois, the strongest man in Valencia County and as brave as any, we stopped "poco tiempo" for lunch which Dan's handsome Mexican wife got for us immediately if not sooner."[78]

Although Dubois was not a major figure of the Indian trade, he was a friend of several of the most significant figures in this commercial endeavor. Dan supplied his little store through the C.N. Cotton Company located in Gallup and although is business was small, he was known for his honesty and for paying his bills on

[76] Judd, Neil M. Men Met Along the Trail Adventures in Archeology. (Norman: Oklahoma University Press, 1968), 107,113-117.

[77] Hannett, Thomas Arthur. Sagebrush Lawyer. (New York: Pageant Press, 1964), 32-34.

Dodge, Black Rock. , 140,141.

Autry, G. Master to F.W. Hodge April 24, 1951.

[78] Lummis, Charles. "Lum and Doc on the Warpath and Loaded for B'ar." Los Angeles Times, September 30, 1887.

Note: At this time McKinley County had not been formed, Gallup and its environs were a part of Valencia County

time.[79] Dan's wife Dorotea worked for many years as a cook and housekeeper for the Cotton family at their home in Gallup, New Mexico.[80] In addition to a close personal relationship with C. N. Cotton, Dan had a long and deep friendship with Cotton's business partner, John Lorenzo Hubbell. [81] Dan's daughter Amelia Dubois Garduno said that Dan had known Hubbell when he was a young boy going to a mission school in Santa Fe.[82] Hodge pointed out that Hubbell and Dubois were employed as mail carriers, taking the mail from Fort Defiance to Fort Apache, for the army. At that time, they used Dan's ranch at Deer Springs as their headquarters.[83] Dan and Hubbell also worked together as Spanish interpreters at the Fort Defiance Agency.[84] Later in life, when Dan fell on hard times both Hubbell and Cotton came to his aid.[85]

Hubbell operated a trading post off the Navajo Reservation, between Gallup and the Zuni Pueblo near Cousins, New Mexico called Pinion Springs, which was located near Dan's place at Pyramid Springs. Hubbell found out that his friend, then in his eighties, was in poor health and arranged for him to live with his store manager, Edward Vanderwagen and his wife Alberdina "Dena" Brink until he recovered his health. [86]

[79] Hodge, "Old Dan DuBois", 145.
[80] Autry, G. Mason to F.W. Hodge August 4, 1952.
[81] Autry, E. Vanderwagen to F.W. Hodge, November 14, 1950.
[82] Autry, A. Garduno to F.W. Hodge November 16, 1950.
[83] Hodge, "Old Dan DuBois", 147.
[84] McNitt, The Indian Traders. , 156
[85] Jeffers, Jo. "Hubbell Trading Post Historic Site". Arizona Highways, September 1967, 4,5,12.
[86] Thomas, Shiwi Vander Wagen. , 21

Dan was well known to the Vanderwagen family. The historian Helen Airy tells of the first meeting of the patriarch of the Vanderwagen family, Andrew and Dubois. Andrew and his wife Effa arrived in Gallup on October 10, 1886, from Grand Rapids, Michigan to begin their work as missionaries only to be met at the train station by a group of mounted cowboys. These men, led by Dan Dubois, met every arriving train and did so to pass judgment on the newly arrived. Because of the increase in mining in the area, the population was increasing and there were issues of mining claims being staked on grazing land used by local ranchers. The good citizens of Gallup had formed a reception committee to meet all in-coming trains and Dan Dubois and the cowboys were to pass judgment; if Dan and the boys thought you were okay, and would benefit the community, than you could stay, if not, it was wise to get on the next train out of town. When Andrew Vanderwagen and his traveling companion Herman Fryling explained that they were planning to preach the Gospel, Dan judged that they were needed in the community. Dan did object to Vanderwagen taking his, "pretty young bride out to the Navajo country to be killed". Dan reportedly said to Vanderwagen, "You don't even have a pistol to protect her." At this, Vanderwagen pulled out a copy of the New Testament, and declared to Dan and his men that the Bible was his six-shooter and delivered a short sermon. Dan was so impressed with Vanerwagen's courage that he and his posse escorted the Vanderwagens and the Fryling's on their journey to Fort

Defiance.[87] Over time, the Vanderwagens say, Andrew tried to convert Dan, but he would always reply by saying, "Well, well, I hope I never go to hell, but I will."[88] Andrew Vanerwagen's first assignment was at Fort Defiance, but he soon was asked to find additional mission sites. He approached his, new friend Dan Dubois about establishing a mission on the Whitewater wash, near Dan's trading post at Pyramid Springs. Dan told Vanderwagen that he would do better to try Zuni.[89]

Edward and Dena Vanderwagen recalled Dan as a fierce looking old man without teeth and having a huge mustache. Dena recollected that although he had a reputation as a hard man, he was very kind and helped people in need.[90] She said that Dan loved to hold their baby and tell stories of his adventures. One story she recalled is how he was wounded in a fracas with Indians, partly scalped and left for dead. The Vanderwagens said that Zane Gray and Harold Bell Wright came to visit Dan but he would not speak with them.

J.L. Hubbell visited the Pinion Springs store often and liked to have lunch with the Vanderwagens and Dan. The Vanderwagens remembered that Hubbell, upon leaving, would always tell Dan to behave like a gentleman because there were ladies in the house. Dan lived with the Vanderwagens for about three months, until he regained

[87] Noe, Sally. Gallup, New Mexico, USA. (Virginia Beach, VA: Donning Company, 1997). , 67, 68.
[88] Airy, Helen L. Whatever Happened to Billy the Kid. (Santa Fe: Sandstone Press, 1993), 102.
[89] Telling, "New Mexico Frontier", 163.
[90] University of New Mexico, Southwest Research Center, Sally Noe Collection 837, BC Box 1.

his health, and once Dan's health had returned, Hubbell set up a small fund to help him meet necessities. [91]

The friendship between Hubbell and Dan Dubois was deep and long-lasting Hubbell at one point told Hodge that he had found Dubois drunk and passed-out in an arroyo at Fort Wingate and had taken Dan home, because he feared that his old friend would die of exposure.[92]

Southwestern writers Martha Blue and Frank McNitt tell a story about how Dan Dubois came to the aid of the Navajo children of trader Curt Cronemeyer.   Cronemeyer operated a trading post south of Gallup, New Mexico not far from Dan's home at Pyramid Springs, but moved to Chambers, Arizona to be nearer the railroad. In June of 1915, he sold a load of wool and other goods in Gallup and returned home with a large amount of cash. Sometime during the night of June 25, 1915, Cronemeyer's store was robbed and both Cronemeyer and his helper Charles Brewer a.k.a Red McDonald were killed.

The double murder and the double funeral that followed were a sensation in Gallup, but the fight over Curt Cronemeyer's $44,000 estate proved to be bitter. Cronemeyer had family in Germany and they claimed his estate, however Curt had been married to two Navajo women and had a son and a daughter. His son Hoskay Cronemeyer contested the German claim.

In December of 1915, in St. Johns, Arizona, the county seat of Apache County an estate proceeding was

[91] Autry, E. Vanderwagen to F.W. Hodge, November 1, 1950.
[92] Hodge, "Old Dan DuBois", 144.

---

held and Dan was on hand to support the Navajo heirs. The court found for the Navajo heirs and appointed Navajo agency superintendent Peter Paquette as guardian for the children. This victory was in no small part due to Dubois's testimony. Others, including J.L. Hubbell, a long time friend of both Dan's and Cronemeyer testified against these heirs stating that Curt Cronemeyer never acknowledged that he had fathered the children. [93]

[93] Blue, Indian Trader, 122.

Dan Dubois or Dennis Donavan

y the early 1920s, Dan was in poor health, living in various places with different family members and was financially indigent. Dan needed help. He received help from many of his friends in Gallup, New Mexico, the town that served as Dan's headquarters since its founding in 1881. Dan had many friends who were prominent citizens of the area, merchants, Indian Traders, and a newspaper editor. Men such as, Clinton Nash Cotton, John Lorenzo Hubbell, Edward Hart, Gregory Page, and Evon Z. Vogt, Sr., editor of *The Gallup Independent*.[94]

With the aid of his friends, he applied for a veterans' pension and admission to the Old Soldiers' Home in Sawtelle, California. In his, application, made on May 1, 1922, in Gallup Dan made the astounding statement that his true name was Dennis Donovan and he had been born somewhere near Santa Barbara in California on March 7, 1835. According to Dan's new account of his life, his parents were James and Julia Donovan. His father, James, was an Irish immigrant and his mother,

---

[94] Hodge, "Old Dan DuBois", 148.

Julia was of French heritage possibly Basque, he was not sure of his mother's maiden name, but thought that it may have been Dubois.

When Dennis was very young, the family made a trip to Ireland, but returned to the United States by way of New York and settled in Steubenville, Ohio. The family prospered in Ohio and to James and Julia several more children were born: William, Jeremiah, and David (who would become a United States Congressman from Ohio, serving from 1891 to 1895) and two girls Ellen and Anna.

Dennis found life in Ohio to be dull and his people too "high toned" and so he ran off at an early age and never returned to his family. For a time he lived in St. Louis and when reaching New Mexico in 1852, Dennis changed his name to Daniel Dubois, taking the surname from a maternal uncle, Leon Dubois, who lived in Los Lunas, New Mexico Territory.[95] He went on to say that as Dan Dubois, he had known nearly every man of note in the west in the "Pioneer Days" and named such figures as mountain men like Jim Beckwith, Jim Baker, and Kit Carson. He also named Governor Alexander Cameron Hunt of Colorado, the Bent brothers, Ben Holladay the stagecoach magnate, and several military notables including Col. John M. Chivington of Glorieta fame and Sand Creek infamy.

Dennis was admitted to the Old Soldiers' Home, and his old friend C.N. Cotton saw him off at the train

[95] A Leon Dubois is found in the U.S. Census for New Mexico in 1860 and 1870; he also served in the Civil War as a Lieutenant in the 1st. Reg. Co. I New Mexico Volunteers. www. fanilysearch.org.

station.[96] At his new home, Dan provided another deposition to G.M. Millburn, a Special Examiner of the Bureau of Pensions in January of 1925. In this document, Donovan (Dan) focused on this military service and his need for care. He also noted that he had not seen his family in Ohio since he left home but that he knew of a brother who had served as a United States Congressman.[97] The Bureau of Pensions had contacted Dennis David Donovan of Napoleon , Ohio who in a written statement said, " I had no relative that I know of named Dennis Donovan, except an uncle who died more than fifty years ago." Mr. Donovan also listed his parents as being-John and Catharine Donovan.[98] In spite of this discrepancy, the Bureau of Pensions awarded Dennis Donovan alias Dan Dubois a pension as a Civil War Veteran and allowed him to remain at the Sawtelle Old Soldiers' Home.[99]

When Dennis was admitted to the institution on December 17, 1923, he suffered from arterial sclerosis and an old fracture of the right leg, which prevented him from walking without a cane. He also had defective vision. On March 13, 1925, Dennis Donovan aka Daniel Dubois died of bilateral bronchi pneumonia and arterial sclerosis. He was buried on March 16, 1925, in the veterans' cemetery at the Sawtelle facility in section 27, row K

[96] Autry, C.N. Cotton to Charles Lummis, January 5, 1924.

[97] Milburn, G.M. "Sworn Statement of Dennis Donovan alias Dan Dubois, at Soldier's Home, Los Angeles, CA", January 2, 1925.

[98] Department of the Interior, Bureau of Pensions, Special Examination Division-1212270. E.B. Olmsted to Dennis D. Donovan, February 3, 1924.

[99] Journal of the U.S. Senate, Sixty-Seventh Congress, Second Session, December 5, 1921, 381,532,600

number 9 under the name Joseph Dubois. C.M. Cotton the son of C.N.Cotton, who was living in Los Angeles at this time, was listed as a friend and contact person. No one can explain why Dennis Donovan aka Dan Dubois was buried under the name Joseph Dubois.[100]

[100] Bartels, Kerry. kerry.bartels@nara.gov" Dennis Donovan" 10 August 2009, Personal e-mail (10 August 2009).
A Joseph Dubois was a Sawtelle patient at the same time as Dan. He was from Rifle, Co. and served in the 40 th Ohio Infantry. He died on March 16, 1925. The deaths of two Dubois so close together may have led to a confusion of identities and Dan being buried under the wrong name.   www.familysearch.org.,   www.   inter-ment.net/data/us/losAngeleses/lanat_d08.htm.

The Life of Dan Dubois: Fact or Fiction

What may be said about the life of Dan Dubois? Was he, as he stated in 1922, Dennis Donovan? If Dan is taken at his word, he was born in California when that state was a part of Mexico and at some point in his childhood, the family traveled to Ireland and returned to the United States and settled in Ohio. However, Donovan statements about his place of birth are not consistent. His Union Navel enlistment record gives his birthplace as Ireland something he denied in his 1922 statement.[101] On the other hand, was Dennis Donovan really Dan Dubois? Nevertheless, even as Dan Dubois, Dennis located his birthplace at various places, in the 1880 U.S. Census his birthplace is given as California. In his 1889 interview with the *Daily New Mexican*, at the Exchange Hotel in Santa Fe, Dan stated that his place of birth was Costillo, Mexico. In the 1920 U.S. Census, he gives his birthplace as Louisiana;[102] to add to the mystery, the account in the *Budget* of 1888 states that Dan Dubois was from Wheeling,

[101] Dubois, Statement Gallup, NM, May 1, 1922.
[102] www. ancestry.com. United States Federal Census, 1880, 1900, 1920.
The Budget. "An Adventure in Zuni", 1889.

West Virginia, when that city was in the state of Virginia. Some of the most basic biographical questions such as where one is born, one's parents cannot be answered in Dan's case due to his careful guarding of his identity during his lifetime.[103] He refused to speak to all who wished to write about him as a hero of the old west, at one time Dan refused to Zane Grey an interview. His old friend Nathan Bibo of St. Johns, Arizona collected considerable information on him with the intent of publishing, but stopped when Dan became angry. Evon Z. Vogt Sr., at Dan's ranch a few days when Vogt was taking the 1920 census, Dan was in full form, during Vogt's visit, telling stories of the old days and Vogt recorded each story in a notebook. At the end of his visit, Dan asked to see the notebook; Vogt passed the book to him and Dubois threw it into the stove without a word.[104] Dan would have agreed with folk singer Bob Dylan, who said in a reflective moment in 2004, "You call yourself what you want to call yourself. This is the land of the free."[105]

However, there are also inconsistencies in Dan Dubois's life that went beyond his name and place of birth. Dan's daughter Amelia Dubois Garduno said that her father's life was a puzzle; he sometimes told me pieces of it.[106] Many of the missing puzzle pieces have to

[103] Telling, "New Mexico Frontier", 27.
[104] Vogt, Evon Sr. "Dan Dubois-Frontier Character" The Gallup Gazette, August 18, 1939.
[105] Linthicum, Leslie, "Did Dylan Roots Really Reach Gallup" Albuquerque Journal, September 13, 2012.
[106] Autry, A. Garduno to F.W. Hodge, June 6, 1950.

do with the stories told about Dan as a scout and Indian fighter and the wounds and scars he gained during these years. Several old timers who knew Dan well spoke of the many scars he had on this body. Edward Vanderwagen said that Dan's body was filled with lead and arrowheads that could be felt under his skin.[107] Evon Vogt, Sr. wrote in the *Gallup Gazette* on August 18, 1939, that Dubois had a scalp wound almost around his head where during a fight with an Apache, Dan's scalp was cut to the bone. Vogt went on to say that, Dubois carried a bullet in this leg and that his leg had been broken during his time with the Utes, which forced Dan to walk with a cane.[108] In 1923, when Dan was admitted to the Old Soldiers' Home in Sawtelle, California his physical examination remarked that he had an old fracture of the right leg, but no other wounds or scars were noted.[109]

Dan's career as a scout provides many puzzle pieces that do not quite fit. A local tale has Dan taking part in General Carleton's Navajo Round-up and places him with Colonel Kit Carson during the Canyon de Chelly campaign. The July 1923 edition of *The Santa Fe Magazine* contains a feature about the dedication of the expansion of the "El Navajo" the Harvey House in Gallup. The article celebrates Dan Dubois as a companion of Kit Carson and Hash-Kay Yashi as the oldest living Navajo medicine man, these two, the author states, "Sixty years before these two engaged in an

[107] Autry, E. Vanderwagen to F.W. Hodge, November 11, 1950.
[108] Vogt, Evon Sr. "Dan Dubois-Frontier Character" The Gallup Gazette, August 18, 1939.
[109] Bartels, e-mail, August 10, 2009.

earnest and persistent effort to shoot each other."
[110]Dan's old friend C.N. Cotton made sure that Dan was
one of the featured old scouts and Indians honored at the
celebration.[111] Cotton may have not been aware that
Dubois as Dennis Donovan was serving in the Union
Army and Navy during the Navajo campaign. Dan's service in the Apache wars was noted in the 1889 issue of
the *Budget* but his name does not appear in the United
States National Archives Old Military Records Index of
Scouts and Guides. Arthur B. House Jr., the National
Archives stated that because Dan Dubois's name does not
appear on the Index does not mean that he did not serve;
it only means that his service was not recorded at the
time of service. In addition, many of the Indian Wars
Quarter Master Records have not been indexed.[112]

The conflict between the sheepmen and cattlemen
in St. Johns, Arizona that boiled over at the fiesta of St. John
the Baptist in June of 1882, and Dan's role in the resulting
gunfight, is another area of mystery. Cameron Udall in
Images of America: St. Johns discusses the shoot out but does
not mention Dubois.[113] Maurice Kildare in an unpublished
work, *The Arizona Sheriff* presents a detailed account of the
conflict from the cattlemen's viewpoint, but does not mention Dan Dubois. Kildare does discuss a powerful man (I

[110] "A Remarkable Indian Ceremony: Navajo Medicine Men Participate
in Unique Housewarming with Rites Centuries Old". Santa Fe Magazine Vol. XVII No. 8. July 1923, 17,18,21,22.
[111] Vogt, The Gallup Gazette, August 18, 1939.
[112] House, Arthur, Interview by John Lewis Taylor (Via telephone) January 26, 2012.
[113] Udall, Images of America:St. Johns , 40,42

assume meaning a powerfully built man) who gives orders to the sheepmen and encourages their attack on the cowboys. From the description, this may be Dubois. Sol Barth is credited by Kildare as the man who braves the gunfire and persuades both sides to end the fight with a promise of a trial.[114] I have found no account of the fiesta day shoot out, other than that of Dan Garduno, which credits Dubois as playing a role in that event.

Dan Garduno thought that Dan enjoyed the mystery. Garduno said, in a 1975 interview that, "Dan Dubois did not think it was anyone's damn business who he was or where he came from." Garduno went on to say that, "He lived his life as Dan Dubois and that man became a legend. I cannot imagine a man named Dennis Donovan becoming a legend. He was a vigorous flamboyant man who paraded himself all over the Southwest and it would have been easier to hide a brass band marching in a parade than to hide Dan Dubois."[115]

Dan Dubois was a man of action, a figure of the Southwest whose life was a mystery and who became a local legend. In his lifetime, he did associate with men of true greatness and influence, men such as: Chief Manuelito, J.L. Hubbell, Frank Hamilton Cushing, Adolph Bandelier, Kit Carson, Lucien Maxwell, and the

[114] Kildare, Maurice. "The Arizona Sheriff" (St. Johns, AZ: Unpublished manuscript in the collection of the Apache   County/St. Johns Family History Center, 1967) 39-43
"Wild Celebration of St. John's Day". News Items of Apache County. " (St. Johns, AZ: Unpublished manuscript in the collection of the Apache County/St. Johns Family History Center, 1967), pages not numbered
[115] Garduno, Interview

Bents. Because Dubois, in his later years did not "grow" his legend, it faded into the dim realm of local memory and he never achieved his place in the pantheon of "Old West" heroes along with William F. Cody or Jack Crawford

Dan Garduno told this story, which seems fitting to focus on the legacy of his grandfather; that once he was having supper with some of his cousins in the Chichiltah area when the talk turned to Dan, Garduno said that Dan Dubois was an old fool for letting so much money slip through his hands, spending it on drink and gambling. At that point, one of the cousins looked up from his bowl of mutton stew and said firmly, "Dan Dubois was good to us, we loved him very much, he fed us when we were hungry-he fed us many times." Garduno said that it was at this point he became a believer in Dan Dubois.[116]

And so may we all be believers in the legend of Dan Dubois, "the last pathfinder and pioneer, who made life easier and softer for those who came after him."[117]

[116] Garduno, Interview
[117] "Dan Dubois, A Path Finder Dies At 91", The Gallup Independent, March 20, 1925.

Epilogue

Dan Dubois lives today in the oral tradition of the people of northwestern New Mexico and northern eastern Arizona. There is no end to the stories told about Dan's exploits. There is the story about the time Dan rode his horse into the Page Hotel bar and bought drinks for the house and there is the time he held a circus ticket-seller at gunpoint until he lowered the price of admission that the poor children of Gallup might see the show. It is also reported that Dan drew his six-gun at a screening of the silent movie, *The Great Train Robbery* and fired back at the desperado holding up the train.[118] Dan's descendants treasure his memory and glory in the exploits of the "Old Frenchman",[119] Gallup's last link with the Wild West.

The official memory of Dan is limited to a pencil sketch portrait drawn from a photo by his great-great grandson Louis Sandoval in the McKinley County courthouse. In a display-case at the Gallup City Hall there is some information about Dan, a brief outline tells the

[118] Link, Interview
[119] Dubois, Sam Bahe, Interview
Kelley, Field Notes KF 0401

Louisiana story of his life and includes some photos, a newspaper article, and a bibliography of books that refer to Dan. The old Santa Fe Railroad Depot, all that is left of Fred Harvey's *El Navajo*, houses the *Gallup Cultural Center* and *Angeles's Café Con Leche,* both display photos of Dan taken at the dedication of the expansion of the El Navajo in 1923. On display at the Navajo Nation museum in Window Rock, Arizona is a photograph by Julian Scott taken in April of 1891,[120] of Chief Manuelito, his wife Juanita, Dan Dubois, his daughter Margaret and other Agency employees and officials of the 11th Special United States Census of Indians Not Taxed, this is the only reference to Dan in the museum

[120] Faris, James C. Navajo and Photography (Albuquerque: University of New Mexico Press, 1996) 86

Dan Dubois 1888: Photo Credit: Braun Research Library, Autry National Center of the American West, Los Angeles; P. 36465

Dan Dubois, Dorotea Ercorcia Dubois, Baby Margaret Dubois, and an Unidentified Woman Photo Credit: Braun Research Library, Autry National Center of the American West, Los Angeles; P. 36462

Dan Dubois and Charles M. Cotton, son of C.N. Cotton. This photo taken at the time Dan entered the Old Soliders Home at Sawtelle, CA. Photo Credit: Braun Research Library, Autry National Center of the American West, Los Angeles; P.36463

Bibliography

Archival Collections

Autry National Center, Braun Research Library, Dan
Dubois Collection, Los Angeles, CA

Bloom Southwest Jewish Archives, Photo Collection,
Tucson, AZ

University of New Mexico, Zimmerman, Center for
Southwest Research, Albuquerque, New Mexico.

Henry County Historical Society, Napoleon, OH

Published Materials

Books

Airy, Helen L. Whatever Happened to Billy the Kid.
Santa Fe: Sunstone Press, 1993

Bender, Norman J. New Hope for the Indians: The
Grant Peace Policy and the Navajo in the 1870s.
Albuquerque: University of New Mexico Press,
1989.

Billington, Monroe Lee. <u>New Mexico's Buffalo Soldiers 1866-1900</u>. Niwot, Colorado: University of Colorado Press, 1991

Blue, Martha. <u>Indian Trader: The Life and Times of J.L. Hubbell</u>. Walnut, California: Kiva Publishing, 2000

Britton, Davis. <u>The Truth About Geronimo</u>. Lincoln: University of Nebraska Press, 1929.

Cozzens, Peter Ed. <u>Eye Witnesses to the Indian Wars, 1865-1890: The Struggle for Apacheria</u>. Mechanicsburg, PA: Stackpole Books, 2001.

Crutchfield, James A. <u>It Happened In Arizona</u>. Globe, AZ: Pequot Press, 1994

Denetdale, Jennifer Nez. <u>Reclaiming Dine' History: The Legacies of Navajo Chief Manuelito and Juanita.</u> Tucson: University of Arizona Press, 2007.

Dodge, William A. <u>Black Rock: A Zuni Cultural Landscape and the Meaning of Place</u>.

Jackson, MS.: University Press of Mississippi, 2007.

Faris, James C. <u>Navajo and Photography: A Critical History of the Representation of an American People.</u> Albuquerque: University of New Mexico Press, 1996

Freiberger, Harriet. <u>Lucien Maxwell Villain or Visionary</u>. Santa Fe: Sunstone Press, 1990

Frink, Maurice. <u>Fort Defiance and the Navajo.</u> Boulder, Co.: Pruett Press, 1968.

Glasrud, Bruce A. and Michael N. Scarles. <u>Buffalo Soldiers in the West: Black Soldiers Anthology.</u> College Station: Texas A. & M. University Press, 2007

Graves, Laura. <u>Thomas Varker Keam Indian Trader</u>. Norman, OK.: Oklahoma University Press, 1998.

Green, Jesse Ed. <u>Cushing At Zuni: The Correspondence and Journals of Frank Hamilton Cushing 1879-1884.</u> Albuquerque: University of New Mexico Press, 1990

Hannett, Thomas Arthur<u>. Sagebrush Lawye</u>r. New York: Pageant Press, 1965.

Hafen, LeRoy R. Ed. <u>Mountain Men and the Fur Traders of the Far West</u>. Lincoln, NE.: University of Nebraska Press, 1965.

Judd, Neil M. <u>Men Meet Along the Trail: Adventures in Archaeology</u>. Norman, OK.: Oklahoma Press, 1968.

Lekson, Stephen N. <u>Nana's Raid.</u> El Paso, TX.: Texas Western Press, 1987.

Locke, Raymond Friday. <u>The Book of the Navajo</u>.

Los Angeles: Mankind Publishing Company, 2001 original, 1976.

Lange, Charles H., Carroll L. Riley and Elizabeth M. Lange. <u>The Southwest Journals of Adolph F. Bandelier 1883-1884</u>. Albuquerque: The University of New Mexico Press, 1970

Lange, Charles H., Carroll L. Riley and Elizabeth M. Lange. <u>The Southwest Journals of Adolph F. Bandelier 1889-1892</u>. Albuquerque: The University of New Mexico Press, 1984.

Miller, Darlis. <u>The California Column in New Mexico</u>. Albuquerque: University of New Mexico Press, 1982.

Miller, Darlis. <u>Jack Crawford Buckskin Poet, Scout and Showman</u>. Albuquerque: University of New Mexico Press, 1993

Moore, William Haas<u>. Chiefs, Agents, and Soldiers</u>. Albuquerque: University of New Mexico Press, 1994.

McNitt, Frank. <u>The Indian Traders</u>.

Norman, OK. : Oklahoma University Press, 1962.

McNitt, Frank<u>. Navajo Wars: Military Campaigns, Slave Raids and Reprisals</u>. Albuquerque: University of New Mexico Press, 1972.

Noe, Sally. <u>Our Gallup, New Mexico U.S.A. Story</u>. Virginia Beach, VA.: The Donning Company, 1997.

Schudert, Frank N. <u>Voices of the Buffalo Soldiers: Records and Recollections of Military Life and Service in the West</u>. Albuquerque: University of New Mexico Press, 2003.

Stevenson, Matilda Coxe. <u>The Zuni Indians</u> Glorieta, NM.: Rio Grande Press, 1970.

Stratton, R.B. Captivity of the Oatman Girls, Being an Interesting Narrative of Life Among the Apache and Mohave Indians. New York: Carlton and Porter, 1857 reprint 1982 from 1857 edition.

Terrell, John Upton. Apache Chronicle New York: World Publishing, 1972

Thomas, Elaine D. Shiwi Vander Wagens Family Memories Zuni, NM.: Self-published, 1997.

Trapp, Dan L. Victorio and the Mimbres Apaches. Norman: Oklahoma University Press, 1974.

Udall, Cameron. Images of American: St. Johns. Charleston, SC.: Arcadia Publishing, 2008.

Wilken, Robert L. Anselm Weber O.F.M. Missionary to the Navajo, 1898-1921. Milwaukee: Bruce Publishing Company, 1955.

Periodicals

Hodge, Fredrick Webb. "Old Dan DuBois." Los Angeles Westerners Brandbook, 1950.

Jeffers, Jo. "Hubbell Trading Post National Historic Site". Arizona Highways, September 1967.

Leaden, Leo R. "Kit Carson's Cave". The Desert Magazine, April 1939

Mifflin, Margot. "Olive Oatman White Mohave". <u>Native Peoples</u>, January/February, 2010

"A Remarkable Indian Ceremony: Navajo Medicine Men Participate in Unique Housewarming with Rites Centuries Old." <u>Santa Fe Magazine</u> Vol. XVII No. 8. July 1923.

Silverman, Jason. "Indian Slavery: The Genizaros in New Mexico". <u>Native Peoples</u>, July/August, 2011.

Newspapers

The Navajo Times. March 2, 1967

The Independent. September 30, 2003

The Gallup Independent. March 20, 1925

The Gallup Independent. February 14, 1916

Albuquerque Journal. September 13, 2012

Los Angeles Times. October 8, 1920 (on-line)

The Gallup Gazette. August 18, 1939

Los Angeles Times. September 30, 1887 (on-line)

Phoenix New Times. March 8, 1989 (on-line)

The Budget. August 20, 1881

The Santa Fe New Mexican Review. September 4, 1884

Interviews

Dubois, Paul (Gallup, NM) Interview with John Lewis Taylor, July 7, 2009

Dubois, Ramona (Grants, NM) Interview with John Lewis Taylor, August 25, 2011

Dubois, Sam Bahe (via telephone) Interview with John Lewis Taylor, June 7, 2010

Garduno, Daniel Dubois (site unknown) Interview with Richard Rubi, form the collection of Rosemarie "Shorty" Sandoval, 1974-1975

Montoya, Mary Ann (Grants, NM) Interview with John Lewis Taylor, August 6, 2012

Juarez, Anthony (Gallup, NM) Interview with John Lewis Taylor, October 16, 2012

Kelley, Klara (Gallup, NM) Interview with John Lewis Taylor, August 5, 2010

Kelley, Klara (Gallup, NM) Interview with John Lewis Taylor, July 17, 2010

Link, Martin (Gallup, NM) Interview with John Lewis Taylor, July 13, 2010

Thomas, Elaine D. (Zuni, NM) Interview with John Lewis Taylor, June 18, 2010

Wilson, Shirley (Gallup, NM) Interview with John Lewis Taylor, July 12, 2010

Freiberger, Harriet (via telephone) Interview with John Lewis Taylor, February 4, 2011

House, Arthur, Jr. (via telephone) Interview with John Lewis Taylor, January 26, 2012

Unpublished Materials

Kelley, Klara and Harris Francis. "Field Notes KF 0401", April 1, 2011

Kelley, Klara. "Miscellaneous Reports on Pyramid Springs" August 23, 2010

Kildare, Maurice. "The Arizona Sheriff" St. Johns, Arizona: Collection of the Apache County/St. Johns Family History Center, 1967

Telling, Irving Jr. "New Mexican Frontiers: A Social History of the Gallup Area, 1881-1901" Doctoral Dissertation, Harvard University, 1953

Tietjen, Gary. "Encounter with the Frontier". Los Alamos: Collection of the Gallup Public Library, 1969

"Wild Celebration of St. John's Day." News Items of Apache County. Collection of the Apache County/St. Johns Family History Center.

E-Mail

Baer, Peggy. < ptbaer@gmail.com> "Dan Notes" 2 August 2009, personal e-mail (2 August 2009)

Denetdale, Jennifer < jdenet@unm.edu> "Rose Manuelito" 30 September 2010, personal e-mail (30 September 2010)

Bartels, Kerry < kerry.bartels@nava.gov> "Dennis Donovan" 10 August 2009, personal e-mail (10 August 2009)

Kelley, Klara < kbkelley47@yahoo.com> "Dan Dubois" 07 January 2012 personal e-mail (07 January 2012)

Kelly, Klara < kbkelley47@yahoo.com> "Review Copy of Dan Dubois" 03 March 2013 personal e-mail (20 March 2013)

Juarez, Anthony < tps50@msn.com> "Rose Manuelito" 23 November 2012 personal e-mail (23 November 2012)

Government Documents

C.B. Hatch to Commissioner of Pensions. Donovan, Dennis Ex Coal Heaver Pension Claim, Bureau of Pensions, July 3, 1924

Declaration of Pension of Dennis Donovan, Bureau of Pensions, October 29, 1924

Drop Report of Pensioner-Invalid 1212270 Dennis Donovan, Bureau of Pension, March 26, 1925

Dubois, Dan. Sworn Statement before a Notary, McKinley County, New Mexico, May 1, 1922

From the collection of Martin Link

G.M. Milburn. Sworn Statement of Dennis Donovan alias Dan Dubois, at Soldiers' Home, Los Angeles, California, January 2, 1925. From the collection of Martin Link

Dubois, Daniel. Homestead Papers. U.S. Department of the Interior, October 22, 1904

Pacific Branch National Home for Disabled Volunteer Soldiers, Report to Commissioner of Pensions Concerning Dennis Donovan, Alias Dan Dubois, March 16, 1925

United States War Department, Volunteer Service, Civil war, Record of Dennis Donovan Civil War Service in the 129th Ohio Volunteer Infantry

Letter from Department of the Interior, Bureau of Pensions to the Hon. Dennis D. Donovan c1212270 with Donovan's reply, February 3, 1924

Journal of the Senate of the United States of America, Second Session of the Sixty-Seventh Congress, December 5, 1921 Washington D.C.: Government Printing Office, 1922

Websites

www.Rubifamilyconnection.com

www.davidrumsey.com/maps5457.html. July 1, 2013

www.Ancestery.com

www.Familysearch.org

www.interment.net/data/us/ca/losangles/lanat_d08.htm.
June 24, 2012.

CPSIA information can be obtained
at www.ICGtesting.com
Printed in the USA
FSOW01n0950110315
5676FS